Life Gave Me You;
I Want to Hear
Your Story

A Guided Journal for
Stepmothers
To Share Their Life Story

Jeffrey Mason

HEAR YOUR
STORY

"Who Needs Fairy Godmothers When There are Stepmoms."

IT'S YOUR BIRTHDAY!

"Becoming a mother doesn't begin at DNA. It happens with the choice to love unconditionally" — Unknown

1. What is your birthdate?

   _____

2. What was your full name at birth?

   _____

3. Were you named after a relative or someone else of significance?

   _____

   _____

   _____

4. In what city were you born?

   _____

   _____

5. Were you born in a hospital? If not, where?

   _____

   _____

6. What was your height (length) and weight at birth?

   _____

   _____

IT'S YOUR BIRTHDAY!

"Families don't have to match. You don't have to look like someone else to love them." — Leigh Anne Tuohy

7. How old were your parents when you were born?

   _____

8. Were you the oldest, middle, or youngest child? How many siblings do you have?

   _____

   _____

   _____

9. What were your first words?

   _____

10. What have your parents told you about how you were as a baby?

    _____

    _____

    _____

    _____

    _____

    _____

    _____

IT'S YOUR BIRTHDAY!

"Life doesn't come with a manual, it comes
with a mother." — Unknown

11. What story have you been told about the day you
were born?

_____

_____

_____

_____

_____

_____

_____

_____

_____

_____

_____

_____

_____

IT'S YOUR BIRTHDAY!

"We worry about what a child will become tomorrow, yet
we forget that they are someone today." — Stacia Tauscher

12. What is a favorite childhood memory?

_____

_____

_____

_____

_____

_____

_____

_____

_____

_____

_____

_____

_____

_____

FAMILY TREE

"The great use of life is to spend it for
something that will outlast it." — William James

My Mother's Great-
Grandmother

My Mother's Great-
Grandfather

My Mother's
Grandmother

My Mother's
Grandfather

My Mother's Mother

My Mother's Father

My Mother

FAMILY TREE

"Life is not a problem to be solved, but a
reality to be experienced." — Soren Kierkegaard

My Father's Great-
Grandmother

My Father's Great-
Grandfather

My Father's
Grandmother

My Father's
Grandfather

My Father's Mother

My Father's Father

My Father

GROWING UP

"Behind every person who believed and
dreamed and thought they could achieve was a
parent who taught them they could." — Tommie Mason

1. Where did you live in your elementary school years?

   _____

   _____

   _____

2. Did you have a nickname?

   _____

3. What was your favorite treat when you were a kid?

   _____

   _____

4. What were your regular chores?

   _____

   _____

   _____

   _____

5. Did you get an allowance? If yes, how much?

   _____

   _____

   _____

GROWING UP
"A stepparent brings to the family new
eyes, a fresh mind, and an open heart."
— Unknown

6. Who was your best friend?

_____

_____

7. What did you do on a typical Saturday when you were
a kid?

_____

_____

_____

_____

_____

_____

8. What do you miss most about being a child?

_____

_____

_____

_____

_____

_____

GROWING UP

"Even though you're growing up, you
should never stop having fun." — Nina Dobrev

9. Describe what you were like when you were a kid.

_____

_____

_____

_____

_____

_____

_____

10. What was the worst trouble you remember getting
    into as a kid?

_____

_____

_____

_____

_____

_____

WHERE HAVE YOU LIVED?

"Anyone can live in a house, but homes are
created with patience, time and love." — Jane Green

List the cities you have lived in during your life.

Include the dates if you can remember them.

_____

_____

_____

_____

_____

_____

_____

_____

_____

_____

_____

_____

_____

_____

THE TEENAGE YEARS

"A child cannot have too many people who love
them and want to help them succeed." — Donna Kaylor

1. How did you dress and style your hair during your
   teens? Do you have any pictures?

   _____

   _____

   _____

   _____

   _____

2. Did you hang out with a group of people or a few
   close friends? Do you still talk to any of them?

   _____

   _____

   _____

   _____

3. In what kind of car did you learn to drive?

   _____

   _____

4. Who taught you to drive?

   _____

   _____

THE TEENAGE YEARS

"If at first you don't succeed, try doing it the way
Mom told you to in the beginning." — Unknown

5. Did you date in high school? Did you have any
    serious relationships in your teen years?

    _____

    _____

6. Did you have a curfew? If yes, what was it?

    _____

7. Did you ever get in trouble for missing your curfew?
    What was your punishment?

    _____

    _____

    _____

    _____

8. Did you go to any school dances? What were they
    like?

    _____

    _____

    _____

    _____

    _____

THE TEENAGE YEARS

"Little children, headache; big children, heartache."
— Italian Proverb

9. What was a common weekend night like during your teens?

_____

_____

_____

_____

_____

_____

10. Knowing all you know now, what advice would you give your teenage self?

_____

_____

_____

_____

_____

_____

_____

THE TEENAGE YEARS

"Having a teenager can cause parents to
wonder about each other's heredity." — Unknown

11. Describe what you were like during your teen years.

_____

_____

_____

_____

_____

_____

_____

_____

12. Write about a favorite memory from your teens.

_____

_____

_____

_____

_____

_____

_____

"There's No Such Thing as too Many Positive Role Models in a Child's Life."

"Family
not by birth
but by
good fortune,
I'm so lucky
to have you
in my life."
- Unknown

WHAT HAPPENED
THE YEAR YOU WERE BORN?

"Parenthood remains the single greatest
preserve of the amateur." — Alvin Toffler

Google the following for the year you were born:

1. What historical events occurred?

_____

_____

_____

_____

2. What movie won the Academy Award for Best
   Picture? Who won Best Actor and Best Actress?

_____

_____

_____

3. What were a few popular movies that came out the
   year you were born?

_____

_____

_____

_____

_____

WHAT HAPPENED
THE YEAR YOU WERE BORN?

"The most important thing in the
World is family and love." — John Wooden

4. What song was on the top of the Billboard charts?

   _____

5. Who was the President of the United States?

   _____

6. What were a few popular television shows?

   _____

   _____

   _____

   _____

7. What were the prices for the following items?
   - A loaf of bread:
   - A gallon of milk:
   - A cup of coffee:
   - A dozen eggs:
   - The average cost of a new home:
   - A first-class stamp:
   - A new car:
   - A gallon of gas:
   - A movie ticket:

WHAT KIND OF STUDENT WERE YOU?

"Education is what remains after one
has forgotten what one learned in school."
— Albert Einstein

1. What did you like and dislike about school?

   _____

   _____

   _____

   _____

2. What grades did you get?

   _____

   _____

3. What were your favorite and least favorite subjects?

   _____

   _____

   _____

4. What was your relationship with your parents like during your high school years?

   _____

   _____

   _____

WHAT KIND OF
STUDENT WERE YOU?

"Children want the same things we want. To laugh,
to be challenged, to be entertained, and delighted."
— Dr. Seuss

5. Did you play any sports? If yes, which ones?

_____

_____

_____

6. Which school activities did you participate in?

_____

_____

_____

_____

_____

7. Is there a teacher or coach that had a significant
   impact on you? What was their biggest influence?

_____

_____

_____

_____

_____

WHAT KIND OF STUDENT WERE YOU?

"We don't stop going to school when we graduate."
— Carol Burnett

8. What are a few of your favorite songs from your high school years?

_____

_____

_____

_____

_____

9. What would you have done differently in school if you knew then what you know now?

_____

_____

_____

_____

_____

_____

_____

_____

WHAT KIND OF
STUDENT WERE YOU?

"In school, you're taught a lesson and then given a test. In life, you're given a test that teaches you a lesson." — Tom Bodett

10. Write about a favorite memory from your high school years.

_____

_____

_____

_____

_____

_____

_____

_____

_____

_____

_____

_____

_____

TRIVIA

"The way I see it, if you want the rainbow,
you gotta put up with the rain." — Dolly Parton

1. What is your favorite flavor of ice cream?

   _____

2. How do you like your coffee?

   _____

3. How do you like your eggs cooked?

   _____

4. If money were not a concern, where would you
   want to live?

   _____

   _____

   _____

   _____

5. Do you still have your tonsils?

   _____

6. What is your shoe size?

   _____

7. How old were you when you started to walk?

   _____

TRIVIA

"Becoming a mother changes everything."
— Adriana Trigiani

8. Do you have any allergies?

_____

_____

_____

9. What superpower would you pick for yourself?

_____

_____

10. What would you pick as your last meal?

_____

_____

_____

_____

_____

11. Preference: cook or clean?

_____

12. Were you a Girl Scout?

_____

YOUR PARENTS

"While we cannot prepare the future for our children, we can prepare our children for the future." — Franklin D. Roosevelt

1. Where was your mother born and where did she grow up?

   _____

   _____

   _____

   _____

2. What three words would you use to describe her?

   _____

   _____

   _____

3. In what ways are you most like your mother?

   _____

   _____

   _____

   _____

   _____

   _____

YOUR PARENTS

"Parents. They didn't leave you when you were young.
So, don't leave them when they are old." — Unknown

4. Where was your father born and where did he grow
up?

_____

_____

_____

_____

5. What three words would you use to describe him?

_____

_____

_____

6. In what ways are you like your father?

_____

_____

_____

_____

_____

_____

YOUR PARENTS

"We never know the love of a parent till we
become parents ourselves." — Henry Ward Beecher

7. How did your parents meet?

_____

_____

_____

_____

_____

8. Describe your parent's relationship.

_____

_____

_____

_____

_____

_____

9. Did either of them have any unique talents?

_____

_____

_____

YOUR PARENTS

"As your kids grow, they may forget what you said, but won't forget how you made them feel." — Kevin Heath

10. What family traditions were passed down from your parents or grandparents?

_____

_____

_____

_____

11. What were your parent's occupations?

_____

_____

_____

12. What other individuals had a major role in helping you grow up? What were their biggest influences?

_____

_____

_____

_____

_____

MEMORIES

"My mother had a great deal of trouble with
me, but I think she enjoyed it." — Mark Twain

What is the best advice your parents gave you?

_____

_____

_____

_____

_____

_____

_____

_____

_____

_____

_____

_____

_____

_____

_____

MEMORIES

"The mother is the one supreme asset of national life;
she is more important by far than the successful statesman,
or businessman, or artist, or scientist." — Theodore Roosevelt

What are a few questions you have always
wanted to ask your parents?

_____

_____

_____

_____

_____

_____

_____

_____

_____

_____

_____

_____

_____

_____

MEMORIES

"Memory is a way of holding on to the things you love, the things you are, the things you never want to lose." — Unknown

What is a favorite memory of your Mother?

_____

_____

_____

_____

_____

_____

_____

_____

_____

_____

_____

_____

_____

_____

MEMORIES

"We don't remember days, we
remember moments." — Unknown

What is a favorite memory of your Father?

_____

_____

_____

_____

_____

_____

_____

_____

_____

_____

_____

_____

_____

_____

"If Parents Can Love Multiple Children, Then Children Can Love Multiple Parents."

"A stepparent
is more
than just
a parent;
they made the
choice to love when
they didn't have to. "
- Unknown

LET'S TALK ABOUT YOU CHOOSING US

"It's amazing how one day someone walks into your life and you can't remember how you ever lived without them." —Unknown

1. How did you meet my parent?

   _____

   _____

   _____

   _____

2. What did you do on your first date?

   _____

   _____

   _____

   _____

3. When did you realize that you wanted your relationship with them to become serious? Was there a specific moment or event?

   _____

   _____

   _____

   _____

LET'S TALK ABOUT
YOU CHOOSING US

"To love a person is to see all their magic, and to
remind them of it when they have forgotten." — Unknown

4. When did you know you wanted to marry them? Was
   there a specific moment or event?

   _____

   _____

   _____

   _____

   _____

5. When did my parent tell you that they had kids?

   _____

   _____

   _____

   _____

   _____

6. What three words describe who you want to be to
   your step kids?

   _____

   _____

   _____

LET'S TALK ABOUT
YOU CHOOSING US

"A stepparent is so much more than just a parent: They made
the choice to love when they didn't have to." — Unknown

7. How did my parent describe each of their kids?

_____

_____

_____

_____

_____

_____

_____

8. What was your first impression of each of us?

_____

_____

_____

_____

_____

_____

_____

LET'S TALK ABOUT
YOU CHOOSING US

"It kills you to see them grow up. But I guess it would
kill you quicker if they didn't." — Barbara Kingsolver

9. What excited you the most about becoming a
stepparent?

_____

_____

_____

_____

_____

10. What were your biggest concerns?

_____

_____

_____

_____

_____

_____

SPIRITUALITY & RELIGION

"I believe the choice to become a mother is the choice to
become one of the greatest spiritual teachers there is."
— Oprah Winfrey

1. Were your parents religious or spiritual when you
   were growing up?

   _____

2. How did your parents express their beliefs?

   _____

   _____

   _____

3. What role does religion or spirituality have in your
   life?

   _____

   _____

   _____

   _____

4. Do you believe in miracles? Have you experienced
   one?

   _____

   _____

   _____

   _____

SPIRITUALITY & RELIGION

"Little souls find their way to you whether
they're from your womb or someone else's."
— Sheryl Crow

5. How have your religious beliefs and practices
changed over the course of your life?

_____

_____

_____

_____

_____

6. Do you pray? If yes, how often and to whom do you
pray?

_____

_____

_____

7. What do you do in moments when times are
challenging, and you need inner strength?

_____

_____

_____

_____

_____

SPIRITUALITY & RELIGION

"The best academy is a mother's knee." — James Russell Lowell

8. What is your current religious or spiritual practice?

_____

_____

_____

_____

_____

_____

_____

9. Which do you think has the most impact on our lives: fate or free will? Why do you feel this way?

_____

_____

_____

_____

_____

_____

_____

SPIRITUALITY & RELIGION

"Love, not DNA, is the bond of parent and child." — Unknown

10. What do you think is the purpose of life?

_____

_____

_____

_____

_____

_____

_____

_____

_____

_____

_____

_____

_____

WORK & CAREER

"Choose a job you love, and you will never
have to work a day in your life" — Confucius

1. When you were a kid, what did you want to be when you grew up?

_____

_____

_____

_____

2. What was your first job?

_____

_____

3. How many jobs have you had during your lifetime? List a few of your favorites.

_____

_____

_____

_____

4. What were your least favorites?

_____

_____

_____

WORK & CAREER

"I'm a great believer in luck, and I find the harder
I work, the more I have of it." — Thomas Jefferson

5. Have you ever wanted to have your own business? If
yes, what kind of business would it be?

_____

_____

_____

6. What are three jobs you would never want to have?

_____

_____

_____

7. Is there a job or profession your parents wanted you
to pursue? If yes, what was it?

_____

_____

8. If you could do any profession, what would it be?
Why?

_____

_____

_____

_____

TRIVIA

"To us, family means putting your arms
around each other and being there." — Barbara Bush

1. Do you read your horoscope?

_____

2. What motivates you in life?

_____

_____

_____

3. What is your biggest big pet peeve?

_____

_____

4. Do you ever buy lottery tickets?

_____

5. What is your favorite season of the year?

_____

6. If you could do any one thing for a day, what would
   it be?

_____

_____

_____

_____

TRIVIA

*"Sweater, n.: garment worn by a child when
its mother is feeling chilly."* — Ambrose Pierce

7. What name would you pick if you had to change
your first name?

   _____

8. Who is your hero? What do you admire about them?

   _____

   _____

   _____

   _____

9. If you could only eat three things for the next year,
with no harm to your health, what would you pick?

   _____

   _____

   _____

10. What do you do better than anyone else in the
family?

   _____

   _____

   _____

   _____

LOVE & ROMANCE

"I saw that you were perfect, and so I loved you. Then I saw
that you were not perfect, and I loved you even more."
— Angelita Lim

1. What was the biggest crush you had when you were
   in high school?

   _____

   _____

   _____

   _____

2. What age were you when you had your first date?

   _____

3. Who was it with and what did you do?

   _____

   _____

   _____

   _____

   _____

4. How old were you when you had your first kiss?

   _____

5. Do you believe in love at first sight?

   _____

LOVE & ROMANCE
"The best thing to hold on to in life is each other."
— Audrey Hepburn

6. Do you believe in soul mates?

_____

7. Have you ever written someone a love poem or song?

_____

8. Do you remember any of the lines? Would you mind sharing them?

_____

_____

_____

_____

_____

9. What is your most romantic memory?

_____

_____

_____

_____

_____

_____

LOVE & ROMANCE

"You know you're in love when you can't fall asleep because reality is finally better than your dreams." — Dr. Seuss

10. What is your opinion of online dating?

_____

_____

_____

11. What are the most important qualities of a successful relationship?

_____

_____

_____

_____

_____

12. What is the biggest way relationships have changed from when you were younger?

_____

_____

_____

_____

_____

LOVE & ROMANCE

"I will never stop trying. Because when you find the one, you never give up." — From the Movie, Crazy, Stupid, Love

13. Write about a time that you were able to get over a broken heart. What helped you move on? What advice would you give someone else going through something similar?

_____

_____

_____

_____

_____

_____

_____

_____

_____

_____

_____

_____

_____

"I don't have stepchildren. I have children who happened to be born before I met them."

"Stepparents are not around to replace a biological parent, rather to augment a child's life experience."
- Azriel Johnson

TRAVEL

"Once a year, go someplace you've never been before."
— Dali Lama

1. Do you have a valid passport?

   _____

2. What is your fantasy vacation?

   _____

   _____

   _____

   _____

   _____

3. Are you a light or heavy packer?

   _____

4. What is the one thing from home you always bring
   with you on a trip?

   _____

   _____

5. When traveling, do you stick to familiar foods or do
   you look for places where the locals eat?

   _____

   _____

   _____

TRAVEL

"Man cannot discover new oceans unless he has
the courage to lose sight of the shore." — Andre Gide

6. What is your favorite travel memory?

_____

_____

_____

_____

_____

_____

_____

_____

7. Write about a travel memory from when you were a
   kid.

_____

_____

_____

_____

_____

_____

TRAVEL BUCKET LIST

"Life is short, and the world is wide."
— Unknown

List the top 10 places you would visit if money and time were no concern. Write about why for each choice.

1. _____

_____

2. _____

_____

3. _____

_____

4. _____

_____

5. _____

_____

TRAVEL BUCKET LIST

"The world is a book, and those who do not travel
read only one page." — Saint Augustine

Continued

6. _____

_____

7. _____

_____

8. _____

_____

9. _____

_____

10. _____

_____

POLITICAL STUFF

"What you teach your children, you
also teach their children." — Unknown

1. How old were you when you voted for the first time?

   _____

2. When was the last time you voted?

   _____

3. How have your political opinions changed over the
   years?

   _____

   _____

   _____

   _____

   _____

   _____

   _____

4. What do you think are the three most serious issues
   facing the country?

   _____

   _____

   _____

POLITICAL STUFF

"Children have never been very good at listening to their elders, but they have never failed to imitate them." — James Baldwin

5. Have you ever taken part in a march or boycott? If no, what issues could motivate you to join one?

_____

_____

_____

_____

6. Who in your family would you guess votes differently than you?

_____

_____

_____

_____

7. Who is your favorite political or historical figure? Why do you admire them?

_____

_____

_____

_____

_____

POLITICAL STUFF

"Politics, it seems to me, has been more concerned with right or left instead of right or wrong." — Richard Armour

8. What are the positive and negative impacts your generation has had on the country and the world?

_____

_____

_____

_____

_____

_____

9. In what ways do you agree and disagree with the political choices of your children's generation.

_____

_____

_____

_____

_____

_____

_____

_____

_____

POLITICAL STUFF

"In politics stupidity is not a handicap."
— Napoleon Bonaparte

10. Who is the best president of your lifetime?

_____

11. If you woke up tomorrow and found yourself in charge of the country, what are the first five things would you create or change?

One:

_____

_____

Two:

_____

_____

Three:

_____

_____

Four:

_____

_____

Five:

_____

_____

SECRETS

"Before I got married, I had six theories about raising children;
now, I have six children and no theories." — John Wilmot

1. Is there ever a time when it is okay to tell a lie?
   What was a time when you felt the need to do so?

   _____

   _____

   _____

   _____

2. Have you ever read someone's private mail, email,
   diary, or journal?

   _____

   _____

3. What is your worst habit? What are you doing to
   change it?

   _____

   _____

   _____

   _____

   _____

   _____

SECRETS

"Mothers hold their children's hands for a
short while, but their hearts forever." — Unknown

4. Have you ever secretly looked through someone's
medicine cabinet?

_____

5. Did you ever skip school?

_____

6. If yes, what did you do during the time you should
have been in class?

_____

_____

_____

7. Write about a regret from your past.

_____

_____

_____

_____

_____

_____

ASSORTED QUESTIONS

"When you have brought up kids, there are memories
you store directly in your tear ducts." —Robert Brault

1. Is there a book you have read more than once?

_____

_____

_____

2. When is the last time you could not stop laughing?
   What was the situation?

_____

_____

_____

_____

3. What tradition or practice from past do you wish
   we did more often?

_____

_____

_____

_____

_____

_____

ASSORTED QUESTIONS

"The only steps in this house are the stair steps and the only half in this house is the half & half creamer." — Al Hodson

4. What accomplishment are you most proud of yourself for achieving?

_____

_____

_____

_____

5. What is the most impulsive thing you have ever done? How did it turn out? Would you do it again?

_____

_____

_____

_____

6. What would a perfect day look like to you?

_____

_____

_____

_____

_____

ASSORTED QUESTIONS

"Insanity is hereditary; you get it from your children."
—Sam Levenson

7. If you could have dinner with any five people who have ever lived, who would you pick? Write about why for each.

_____

_____

_____

_____

_____

8. What accomplishment are you most proud of yourself for achieving?

_____

_____

_____

_____

9. Were you ever in a relationship with someone your parents didn't like?

_____

_____

_____

_____

ASSORTED QUESTIONS

"Life is like riding a bicycle. To keep your
balance, you must keep moving." — Albert Einstein

10. If you could only pick one, would you choose to be
in love or rich?

_____

_____

11. What was the most rewarding and the hardest part
of being a mother?

_____

_____

_____

_____

_____

12. Are you an introvert or extrovert?

_____

13. What is your favorite thing about yourself?

_____

_____

_____

_____

_____

70

"You don't choose
your family.
They are
God's gift
to you,
as you are to them."
-Desmond Tutu

"Family
isn't something
that's
supposed
to be
static or set.
It's always
evolving,
turning into
something else."
- Sarah Dessen

TRIVIA

"I really learned it all from mothers." — Benjamin Spock

1. What would be the title of your autobiography?

   _____

   _____

   _____

2. Do you think you could still pass the written portion of the driver's test without studying?

   _____

3. What is your favorite quote?

   _____

   _____

   _____

   _____

4. Do you believe in life on other planets?

   _____

5. If you were forced to sing karaoke, what song would you pick to perform?

   _____

   _____

   _____

TRIVIA

"My daughter introduced me to myself." — Beyoncé Knowles

6. What is your favorite color?

_____

7. What is the first movie you can remember seeing?

_____

_____

8. Who was your role model growing up? What impact did they have on you?

_____

_____

_____

_____

_____

_____

9. When was the last time a movie or something on television made you cry? What was it?

_____

_____

_____

MOVIES, MUSIC, TELEVISION, & BOOKS

"The soul is healed by being with children."
— Fyodor Dostoevsky

1. What movie do you think you have watched the greatest number of times?

   _____

   _____

2. What is a movie you can remember loving when you were a kid?

   _____

   _____

3. Who would you cast to play yourself in the movie of your life? How about the rest of your family?

   _____

   _____

   _____

   _____

   _____

   _____

   _____

   _____

MOVIES, MUSIC, TELEVISION, & BOOKS

"Mom - the person most likely to write an autobiography
and never mention herself." — Robert Breault

4. What are your favorite genres of music?

_____

_____

_____

_____

5. Which decades had the best music?

_____

_____

_____

_____

6. What is the first record, album, cassette, or tape you
remember buying

_____

_____

7. What song do you like today that would make your
younger self cringe?

_____

_____

MOVIES, MUSIC, TELEVISION, & BOOKS

"A mother is not a person to lean on, but a person to make leaning unnecessary." — Dorothy Canfield Fisher

8. What was the first concert you attended? What year did it occur?

_____

_____

9. How has your taste in music changed over the years?

_____

_____

_____

_____

10. What is the first song you can remember loving?

_____

_____

_____

11. What song would you pick as the theme song of your life?

_____

_____

_____

MOVIES, MUSIC, TELEVISION, & BOOKS

"Being a mother means that your heart is no longer yours; it wanders wherever your children do." — George Bernard Shaw

12. What television show from the past do you wish was still on the air?

_____

_____

13. If you could be on any television show or movie, past or present, which one would you pick?

_____

_____

14. What is a favorite book from your childhood or teen years?

_____

_____

15. What book or books have positively impacted the way you think, work, or live your life?

_____

_____

_____

_____

_____

TOP TEN MOVIES

"Mother's Day is the reason Alexander
Graham Bell invented the telephone." —Unknown

List Your Ten Most Favorite Movies:

1. _____

2. _____

3. _____

4. _____

5. _____

6. _____

7. _____

8. _____

9. _____

10. _____

TOP TEN SONGS

"Each day of our lives we make deposits in
the memory banks of our children." —Charles R. Swindoll

List Your Ten Most Favorite Songs:

1. _____

2. _____

3. _____

4. _____

5. _____

6. _____

7. _____

8. _____

9. _____

10. _____

ADVICE

"Children are likely to live up to what
you believe of them." — Lady Bird Johnson

Based upon what you have learned and experienced, in
your life, what is the one piece of advice you would give
your children?

_____

_____

_____

_____

_____

_____

_____

_____

_____

_____

_____

_____

HOW WOULD YOU LIKE TO BE REMEMBERED?

"Children are not only innocent and curious but also optimistic and joyful and essentially happy. They are, in short, everything adults wish they could be." — Carolyn Haywood

How would you like to your family and friends to remember you?

_____

_____

_____

_____

_____

_____

_____

_____

_____

_____

_____

NOTES TO THOSE I LOVE

"Just when you think you know love, something little comes along and reminds you just how big it is." — Unknown

This is space for you to write notes to your loved ones:

_____

_____

_____

_____

_____

_____

_____

_____

_____

_____

_____

_____

NOTES TO THOSE I LOVE

"When you have brought up kids, there are memories
you store directly in your tear ducts." — Robert Brault

This is space for you to write notes to your loved ones:

_____

_____

_____

_____

_____

_____

_____

_____

_____

_____

_____

_____

_____

NOTES TO THOSE I LOVE

"Children are like wet cement: whatever
falls on them makes an impression." — Haim Ginott

This is space for you to write notes to your loved ones:

_____

_____

_____

_____

_____

_____

_____

_____

_____

_____

_____

_____

_____

NOTES TO THOSE I LOVE

"Let me love you a little more before
you're not little anymore." — Unknown

This is space for you to write notes to your loved ones:

_____

_____

_____

_____

_____

_____

_____

_____

_____

_____

_____

_____

_____

_____

NOTES TO THOSE I LOVE
"Of all the things my hands have held,
the best, by far, is you." — Unknown

This is space for you to write notes to your loved ones:

_____

_____

_____

_____

_____

_____

_____

_____

_____

_____

_____

_____

NOTES TO THOSE I LOVE

"The greatest gifts you can give your children are the roots of
responsibility and the wings of independence." — Denis Waitley

This is space for you to write notes to your loved ones:

_____

_____

_____

_____

_____

_____

_____

_____

_____

_____

_____

_____

_____

_____

_____

_____

MOVIES & TV SHOWS
ABOUT BLENDED FAMILIES

"Life is a succession of lessons which
must be lived to be understood."— Helen Keller

- The Big Cat (1949)

- Mary Poppins (1964)

- Yours, Mine, and Ours (1968)

- The Brady Bunch (Television 1969-1974)

- Aristocrats (1970)

- Freaky Friday (1976)

- Diff'rent Strokes (Television 1978-1986)

- Webster (Television 1983-1987)

- Three Men and a Baby (1987)

- Baby Boom (1987)

- My Two Dads (Television 1987 to 1990)

- Full House (Tele vision 1987-1995)

- Parenthood (1989)

- Step by Step (Television 1991-1998)

- Mrs. Doubtfire (1993)

- Sister, Sister (Television 1994-1999)

- Man of the House (1995)

- The Brady Bunch Movie (1995)

- Fly Away Home (1996)

- Stepmom (1998)

MOVIES & TV SHOWS
ABOUT BLENDED FAMILIES

"If evolution really works, how come
mothers only have two hands?" —Milton Berle

- Big Daddy (1999)

- Frequency (2000)

- The Royal Tenenbaums (2001)

- Love Actually (2003)

- Daddy Day Care (2003)

- Freaky Friday (2003)

- Elf (2003)

- Finding Nemo (2003)

- Cheaper by the Dozen (2003)

- Two and a Half Men (Television 2003-2015)

- Jersey Girl (2004)

- Raising Helen (2004)

- Drake & Josh (Television, 2004-2007)

- Your, Mine, & Ours (2005)

- The Pursuit of Happiness (2006)

- The Game Plan (2007)

- Are We Done Yet? (2007)

- Modern Family (Television 2009-2020)

- Despicable Me (2010)

- The Spy Next Door (2010)

MOVIES & TV SHOWS
ABOUT BLENDED FAMILIES

"How ever motherhood comes to you, it's a miracle."
— Valerie Harper

- The Descendants (2011)

- We Bought a Zoo (2011)

- Shameless (Television 2011-2021)

- Big Mommas: Like Father, Like Son (2011)

- Journey 2: The Mysterious Island (2012)

- Sofia the First (Television 2012-2018)

- Instructions Not Included (2013)

- Instant Mom (2013-2015)

- Despicable Me 2 (2013)

- The Fosters (Television 2013-2018)

- The Flash (Television 2014-)

- Blended (2014)

- Maggie's Plan (2015)

- Daddy's Home (2015)

- Fathers and Daughters (2015)

- This Is Us (Television 2016-2020)

- Daddy's Home 2 (2017)

- Mary Poppins Returns (2018)

- The Secret Garden (2020)

- Little America (Television 2020-)

SONGS THAT SHOW WHAT IT MEANS TO BE A STEPMOM

"Children need models rather than critics."
—Joseph Joubert

- The Shirelles, "Mama Said" (1960)

- Ben E. King, "Stand By Me" (1961)

- Beach Boys, "God Only Knows" (1966)

- Crosby, Stills & Nash, "Teach Your Children" (1970)

- The Beatles, "Julia" (1970)

- The Jackson 5, "I'll Be There" (1970)

- Carole King, "Where You Lead, I Will Follow" (1971)

- Carole King, ""You've Got a Friend" (1971)

- Bill Withers, "Lean on Me" (1972)

- Abba, "Does Your Mother Know" (1979)

- Sister Sledge, "We Are Family" (1979)

- Kenny Rogers, "Through the Years" (1981)

- "Tomorrow" from Annie (1982)

- Bette Midler, "Wind Beneath My Wings" (1988)

- Ricky Skaggs, "Thanks Again" (1988)

- The Judds, "Love Can Build a Bridge (1990)

- Madonna, "Promise to Try" (1991)

- Mariah Carey, "Hero" (1993)

- The Pretenders, "I'll Stand By You" (1994)

- Faith Hill, "You Can't Lose Me" (1995)

SONGS THAT SHOW WHAT IT MEANS TO BE A STEPMOM

"My mama always said, life is like a box of chocolates. You never know what you're gonna get." — Forrest Gump

- Jim Rule, "A Family is What You Make It (1995)

- Celine Dion, "Because You Loved Me" (1996)

- Garth Brooks, "A Friend to Me" (1997)

- Backstreet Boys, "The Perfect Fan" (1999)

- Jessica Andrews, "I'll Be There For You" (1999)

- Reba McEntire, "I'll Be" (1999)

- Good Charlotte, "Thank You Mom" (2000)

- Dido, "Thank You" (2000)

- Lee Ann Womack, "I Hope You Dance" (2000)

- Ben Folds, "The Luckiest" (2001)

- Molly Pasutti, "I'm Blessed to Call You Mother" (2001)

- Josh Groban, "You Raise Me Up" (2002)

- Jamie O'Neal, "Somebody's Hero" (2005)

- Rascal Flats, "My Wish" (2006)

- Carrie Underwood, "I'll Stand By You" (2007)

- Sarah Buxton, "Wings" (2010)

- Meghan Trainor, "Mom" (2016)

- "Anybody Have a Map" from Dear Evan Hansen (2017)

- LeeAnn Rimes, "Mother" (2017)

About This Book

They have many names and titles.

Stepmom. Stepmother. Mother. Mom. Bonus Parent. We often just refer to them by their first name.

Whatever we call them, we see what they have brought to our lives.

A stepparent's love is unique because it is completely based on choice.

They chose us.

Their love for another person was so big and unconditional that it had room enough for an entire family with their histories, and traditions, and stories.

They had to find right way to be a parent without being the parent.

They couldn't just rely on rules and orders and discipline. Their way had to be one of listening, teaching, supporting, and encouraging.

Little by little we found ourselves seeing them for who they are instead of who they are not. We found their love and we felt their care and then one day, we chose them.

Just like they chose us.

And because of that, all of us will never be the same.

About the Author

Jeffrey Mason has spent twenty-plus years working with individuals, couples, and organizations to create change, achieve goals, and strengthen relationships.

He begins with the understanding that being human is hard. Jeffrey is fiercely committed to helping others understand that forgiveness is the greatest gift we can give others and ourselves and to remember that while we have eternity, we don't have forever.

Jeffrey would be grateful if you would help people find his books by leaving a review on Amazon. Your feedback helps him get better at this thing he loves.

You can contact him at hello@jeffreymason.com. He would love to hear from you.

The Hear Your Story
Line of Books

At **Hear Your Story**, we have created a line of books focused on giving each of us a place to tell the unique story of who we are, where we have been, and where we are going.

Sharing and hearing the stories of the people in our lives creates communication, closeness, understanding, and the cement of a forever bond.

- Dad, I Want to Hear Your Story; A Father's Guided Journal to Share His Life & His Love

- Mom, I Want to Hear Your Story; A Mother's Guided Journal to Share Her Life & Her Love

- You Chose to Be My Dad; I Want to Hear Your Story: A Guided Journal for Stepdads to Share Their Life Story

- Life Gave Me You; I Want to Hear Your Story: A Guided Journal for Stepmothers to Share Their Life Story

Available at Amazon and all Bookstores

The Hear Your Story Line of Books

- Grandmother, I Want to Hear Your Story: A Grandmother's Guided Journal to Share Her Life and Her Love

- Grandfather, I Want to Hear Your Story: A Grandfather's Guided Journal to Share His Life and His Love

- Dad Notes: Dad, I Wrote This Book for You

- Mom Notes: I Wrote This Book About the Best Mother Ever

- Because I Love You: The Couple's Bucket List That Builds Your Relationship

- Love Notes: I Wrote This Book About You

- Our Story: A Couple's Guided Journal

- You, Me, and Us: 229 Fun Relationship Questions to Ask Your Guy or Girl

- Papá, quiero oír tu historia: El diario guiado de un padre Para compartir su vida y su amor

HEAR YOUR
STORY

Available at Amazon and all Bookstores

Online access to this book can be purchased at www.hearyourstory.com.

This provides you with the ability to answer the questions in this book with a computer, tablet, or smartphone and print multiple copies to give to your entire family.

CPSIA information can be obtained
at www.ICGtesting.com
Printed in the USA
BVHW011838110521
607064BV00002B/82

The Constitution
of the United States

 ## The Declaration of Independence

&

The Bill of Rights

Index

The Declaration of Independence
Action of Second Continental Congress,
July 4, 1776.

The unanimous Declaration of the thirteen united States of America,

When in the Course of human events, it becomes necessary for one people to dissolve the political bands which have connected them with another, and to assume among the powers of the earth, the separate and equal station to which the Laws of Nature and of Nature's God entitle them, a decent respect to the opinions of mankind requires that they should declare the causes which impel them to the separation.

We hold these truths to be self-evident, that all men are created equal, that they are endowed by their Creator with certain unalienable Rights, that among these are Life, Liberty and the pursuit of Happiness.--That to secure these rights, Governments are instituted among Men, deriving their just powers from the consent of the governed, --That whenever any Form of Government becomes destructive of these ends, it is the Right of the People to alter or to abolish it, and to institute new Government, laying its foundation on such principles and organizing its powers in such form, as to them shall seem most likely to effect their Safety and Happiness. Prudence, indeed, will dictate that Governments long established should not be changed for light and transient causes; and accordingly all experience hath shewn, that mankind are more disposed to suffer, while evils are sufferable, than to right themselves by abolishing the forms to which they are accustomed. But when a long train of abuses and usurpations, pursuing invariably the same Object evinces a design to reduce them under absolute Despotism, it is their right, it is their duty, to throw off such Government, and to provide new Guards for their future security.--Such has been the patient sufferance of these Colonies; and such is now the necessity which constrains them to alter their former Systems of Government. The history of the present King of Great Britain is a history of repeated injuries and usurpations, all having in direct object the establishment of an absolute Tyranny over these States. To prove this, let Facts be submitted to a candid world.

He has refused his Assent to Laws, the most wholesome and necessary for the public good.

He has forbidden his Governors to pass Laws of immediate and pressing importance, unless suspended in their operation till his Assent should be obtained; and when so suspended, he has utterly neglected to attend to them.

He has refused to pass other Laws for the accommodation of large districts of people, unless those people would relinquish the right of Representation in the Legislature, a right inestimable to them and formidable to tyrants only.

He has called together legislative bodies at places unusual, uncomfortable, and distant from the depository of their public Records, for the sole purpose of fatiguing them into compliance with his measures.

He has dissolved Representative Houses repeatedly, for opposing with manly firmness his invasions on the rights of the People.

He has refused for a long time, after such dissolutions, to cause others to be elected; whereby the Legislative powers, incapable of Annihilation, have returned to the People at large for their exercise; the State remaining in the mean time exposed to all the dangers of invasion from without, and convulsions within.

He has endeavoured to prevent the population of these States; for that purpose obstructing the Laws for Naturalization of Foreigners; refusing to pass others to encourage their migrations hither, and raising the conditions of new Appropriations of Lands.

He has obstructed the Administration of Justice, by refusing his Assent to Laws for establishing Judiciary powers.

He has made Judges dependent on his Will alone, for the tenure of their offices, and the amount and payment of their salaries.

He has erected a multitude of New Offices, and sent hither swarms of Officers to harrass our people, and eat out their substance.

He has kept among us, in times of peace, Standing Armies without the Consent of our legislatures.

He has affected to render the Military independent of and superior to the Civil power.

He has combined with others to subject us to a jurisdiction foreign to our constitution, and unacknowledged by our laws; giving his Assent to their Acts of pretended Legislation:

For Quartering large bodies of armed troops among us:
For protecting them, by a mock Trial, from punishment for any Murders which they should commit on the Inhabitants of these States:
For cutting off our Trade with all parts of the world:

For imposing Taxes on us without our Consent:

For depriving us in many cases, of the benefits of Trial by Jury:

For transporting us beyond Seas to be tried for pretended offences:

For abolishing the free System of English Laws in a neighbouring Province, establishing therein an Arbitrary government, and enlarging its Boundaries so as to render it at once an example and fit instrument for introducing the same absolute rule into these Colonies:

For taking away our Charters, abolishing our most valuable Laws, and altering fundamentally the Forms of our Governments:

For suspending our own Legislatures, and declaring themselves invested with power to legislate for us in all cases whatsoever.

He has abdicated Government here, by declaring us out of his Protection and waging War against us.

He has plundered our seas, ravaged our Coasts, burnt our towns, and destroyed the lives of our people.

He is at this time transporting large Armies of foreign Mercenaries to compleat the works of death, desolation and tyranny, already begun with circumstances of Cruelty &

perfidy scarcely paralleled in the most barbarous ages, and totally unworthy the Head of a civilized nation.

He has constrained our fellow Citizens taken Captive on the high Seas to bear Arms against their Country, to become the executioners of their friends and Brethren, or to fall themselves by their Hands.

He has excited domestic insurrections amongst us, and has endeavoured to bring on the inhabitants of our frontiers, the merciless Indian Savages, whose known rule of warfare, is an undistinguished destruction of all ages, sexes and conditions.

In every stage of these Oppressions We have Petitioned for Redress in the most humble terms: Our repeated Petitions have been answered only by repeated injury. A Prince whose character is thus marked by every act which may define a Tyrant, is unfit to be the Ruler of a free People.

Nor have We been wanting in attentions to our Brittish brethren. We have warned them from time to time of attempts by their legislature to extend an unwarrantable jurisdiction over us. We have reminded them of the circumstances of our emigration and settlement here. We have appealed to their native justice and magnanimity, and we have conjured them by the ties of our common kindred to disavow these usurpations, which, would inevitably interrupt our connections and correspondence. They too have been deaf to the voice of justice and of consanguinity.

We must, therefore, acquiesce in the necessity, which denounces our Separation, and hold them, as we hold the rest of mankind, Enemies in War, in Peace Friends.

We, therefore, the Representatives of the united States of America, in General Congress, Assembled, appealing to the Supreme Judge of the world for the rectitude of our intentions, do, in the Name, and by Authority of the good People of these Colonies, solemnly publish and declare, That these United Colonies are, and of Right ought to be Free and Independent States; that they are Absolved from all Allegiance to the British Crown, and that all political connection between them and the State of Great Britain, is and ought to be totally dissolved; and that as Free and Independent States, they have full Power to levy War, conclude Peace, contract Alliances, establish Commerce, and to do all other Acts and Things which Independent States may of right do. And for the support of this Declaration, with a firm reliance on the protection of divine Providence, we mutually pledge to each other our Lives, our Fortunes and our sacred Honor.

Georgia
Button Gwinnett
Lyman Hall
George Walton

North Carolina
William Hooper
Joseph Hewes
John Penn

South Carolina
Edward Rutledge
Thomas Heyward, Jr.
Thomas Lynch, Jr.
Arthur Middleton

Massachusetts
John Hancock

Maryland
Samuel Chase
William Paca
Thomas Stone
Charles Carroll of
Carrollton

Virginia
George Wythe
Richard Henry Lee
Thomas Jefferson
Benjamin Harrison
Thomas Nelson, Jr.
Francis Lightfoot Lee
Carter Braxton

Pennsylvania
Robert Morris
Benjamin Rush
Benjamin Franklin
John Morton
George Clymer
James Smith
George Taylor
James Wilson
George Ross

Delaware
Caesar Rodney
George Read
Thomas McKean

New York

William Floyd

Philip Livingston

Francis Lewis

Lewis Morris

New Jersey

Richard Stockton

John Witherspoon

Francis Hopkinson

John Hart

Abraham Clark

New Hampshire

Josiah Bartlett

William Whipple

Massachusetts

Samuel Adams

John Adams

Robert Treat Paine

Elbridge Gerry

Rhode Island

Stephen Hopkins

William Ellery

Connecticut

Roger Sherman

Samuel Huntington

William Williams

Oliver Wolcott

New Hampshire

Matthew Thornton

The Constitution of the United States

We the People of the United States, in Order to form a more perfect Union, establish Justice, insure domestic Tranquility, provide for the common defence, promote the general Welfare, and secure the Blessings of Liberty to ourselves and our Posterity, do ordain and establish this Constitution for the United States of America.

Article. I.

Section. 1.

All legislative Powers herein granted shall be vested in a Congress of the United States, which shall consist of a Senate and House of Representatives.

Section. 2.

The House of Representatives shall be composed of Members chosen every second Year by the People of the several States, and the Electors in each State shall have the Qualifications requisite for Electors of the most numerous Branch of the State Legislature.

No Person shall be a Representative who shall not have attained to the Age of twenty five Years, and been seven Years a Citizen of the United States, and who shall not, when elected, be an Inhabitant of that State in which he shall be chosen.

Representatives and direct Taxes shall be apportioned among the several States which may be included within this Union, according to their respective Numbers, which shall be determined by adding to the whole Number of free Persons, including those bound to Service for a Term of Years, and excluding Indians not taxed, three fifths of all other Persons. The actual Enumeration shall be made within three Years after the first Meeting of the Congress of the United States, and within every subsequent Term of ten Years, in such Manner as they shall by Law direct. The Number of Representatives shall not exceed one for every thirty Thousand, but each State shall have at Least one Representative; and until such enumeration shall be made, the State of New Hampshire shall be entitled to chuse three, Massachusetts eight, Rhode-Island and Providence Plantations one, Connecticut five, New-York six, New Jersey four, Pennsylvania eight, Delaware one, Maryland six, Virginia ten, North Carolina five, South Carolina five, and Georgia three.

When vacancies happen in the Representation from any State, the Executive Authority thereof shall issue Writs of Election to fill such Vacancies.

The House of Representatives shall chuse their Speaker and other Officers; and shall have the sole Power of Impeachment.

Section. 3.

The Senate of the United States shall be composed of two Senators from each State, chosen by the Legislature thereof, for six Years; and each Senator shall have one Vote.

Immediately after they shall be assembled in Consequence of the first Election, they shall be divided as equally as may be into three Classes. The Seats of the Senators of the first Class shall be vacated at the Expiration of the second Year, of the second Class at the Expiration of the fourth Year, and of the third Class at the Expiration of the sixth Year, so that one third may be chosen every second Year; and if Vacancies happen by Resignation, or otherwise, during the Recess of the Legislature of any State, the Executive thereof may make temporary Appointments until the next Meeting of the Legislature, which shall then fill such Vacancies.

No Person shall be a Senator who shall not have attained to the Age of thirty Years, and been nine Years a Citizen of the United States, and who shall not, when elected, be an Inhabitant of that State for which he shall be chosen.

The Vice President of the United States shall be President of the Senate, but shall have no Vote, unless they be equally divided.

The Senate shall chuse their other Officers, and also a President pro tempore, in the Absence of the Vice President, or when he shall exercise the Office of President of the United States.

The Senate shall have the sole Power to try all Impeachments. When sitting for that Purpose, they shall be on Oath or Affirmation. When the President of the United States is tried, the Chief Justice shall preside: And no Person shall be convicted without the Concurrence of two thirds of the Members present.

Judgment in Cases of Impeachment shall not extend further than to removal from Office, and disqualification to hold and enjoy any Office of honor, Trust or Profit under the United States: but the Party convicted shall nevertheless be liable and subject to Indictment, Trial, Judgment and Punishment, according to Law.

Section. 4.

The Times, Places and Manner of holding Elections for Senators and Representatives, shall be prescribed in each State by the Legislature thereof; but the Congress may at any time by Law make or alter such Regulations, except as to the Places of chusing Senators.

The Congress shall assemble at least once in every Year, and such Meeting shall be on the first Monday in December, unless they shall by Law appoint a different Day.

Section. 5.

Each House shall be the Judge of the Elections, Returns and Qualifications of its own Members, and a Majority of each shall constitute a Quorum to do Business; but a smaller Number may adjourn from day to day, and may be authorized to compel the Attendance of absent Members, in such Manner, and under such Penalties as each House may provide.

Each House may determine the Rules of its Proceedings, punish its Members for disorderly Behaviour, and, with the Concurrence of two thirds, expel a Member.

Each House shall keep a Journal of its Proceedings, and from time to time publish the same, excepting such Parts as may in their Judgment require Secrecy; and the Yeas and Nays of the Members of either House on any question shall, at the Desire of one fifth of those Present, be entered on the Journal.

Neither House, during the Session of Congress, shall, without the Consent of the other, adjourn for more than three days, nor to any other Place than that in which the two Houses shall be sitting.

Section. 6.

The Senators and Representatives shall receive a Compensation for their Services, to be ascertained by Law, and paid out of the Treasury of the United States. They shall in all Cases, except Treason, Felony and Breach of the Peace, be privileged from Arrest during their Attendance at the Session of their respective Houses, and in going to and returning from the same; and for any Speech or Debate in either House, they shall not be questioned in any other Place.

No Senator or Representative shall, during the Time for which he was elected, be appointed to any civil Office under the Authority of the United States, which shall have been created, or the Emoluments whereof shall have been encreased during such time; and no Person holding any Office under the United States, shall be a Member of either House during his Continuance in Office.

Section. 7.

All Bills for raising Revenue shall originate in the House of Representatives; but the Senate may propose or concur with Amendments as on other Bills.

Every Bill which shall have passed the House of Representatives and the Senate, shall, before it become a Law, be presented to the President of the United States; If he approve; he shall sign it, but if not he shall return it, with his Objections to that House in which it shall have originated, who shall enter the Objections at large on their Journal, and proceed to reconsider it. If after such Reconsideration two thirds of that House shall agree to pass the Bill, it shall be sent, together with the Objections, to the other House, by which it shall likewise be reconsidered, and if approved by two thirds of that House, it shall become a Law. But in all such Cases the Votes of both Houses shall be determined by yeas and Nays, and the Names of the Persons voting for and against the Bill shall be entered on the Journal of each House respectively. If any Bill shall not be returned by the President within ten Days (Sundays excepted) after it shall have been presented to him, the Same shall be a Law, in like Manner as if he had signed it, unless the Congress by their Adjournment prevent its Return, in which Case it shall not be a Law.

Every Order, Resolution, or Vote to which the Concurrence of the Senate and House of Representatives may be necessary (except on a question of Adjournment) shall be presented to the President of the United States; and before the Same shall take Effect, shall be approved by him, or being disapproved by him, shall be repassed by two thirds of the Senate and House of Representatives, according to the Rules and Limitations prescribed in the Case of a Bill.

Section. 8.

The Congress shall have Power To lay and collect Taxes, Duties, Imposts and Excises, to pay the Debts and provide for the common Defence and general Welfare of the United States; but all Duties, Imposts and Excises shall be uniform throughout the United States;

To borrow Money on the credit of the United States;

To regulate Commerce with foreign Nations, and among the several States, and with the Indian Tribes;

To establish an uniform Rule of Naturalization, and uniform Laws on the subject of Bankruptcies throughout the United States;

To coin Money, regulate the Value thereof, and of foreign Coin, and fix the Standard of Weights and Measures;

To provide for the Punishment of counterfeiting the Securities and current Coin of the United States;

To establish Post Offices and post Roads;

To promote the Progress of Science and useful Arts, by securing for limited Times to Authors and Inventors the exclusive Right to their respective Writings and Discoveries;

To constitute Tribunals inferior to the supreme Court;

To define and punish Piracies and Felonies committed on the high Seas, and Offences against the Law of Nations;

To declare War, grant Letters of Marque and Reprisal, and make Rules concerning Captures on Land and Water;

To raise and support Armies, but no Appropriation of Money to that Use shall be for a longer Term than two Years;

To provide and maintain a Navy;

To make Rules for the Government and Regulation of the land and naval Forces;

To provide for calling forth the Militia to execute the Laws of the Union, suppress Insurrections and repel Invasions;

To provide for organizing, arming, and disciplining, the Militia, and for governing such Part of them as may be employed in the Service of the United States, reserving to the States respectively, the Appointment of the Officers, and the Authority of training the Militia according to the discipline prescribed by Congress;

To exercise exclusive Legislation in all Cases whatsoever, over such District (not exceeding ten Miles square) as may, by Cession of particular States, and the Acceptance of Congress, become the Seat of the Government of the United States, and to exercise like Authority over all Places purchased by the Consent of the Legislature of the State in which the Same shall be, for the Erection of Forts, Magazines, Arsenals, dock-Yards, and other needful Buildings;
—And

To make all Laws which shall be necessary and proper for carrying into Execution the foregoing Powers, and all other Powers vested by this Constitution in the Government of the United States, or in any Department or Officer thereof.

Section. 9.

The Migration or Importation of such Persons as any of the States now existing shall think proper to admit, shall not be prohibited by the Congress prior to the Year one thousand eight hundred and eight, but a Tax or duty may be imposed on such Importation, not exceeding ten dollars for each Person.

The Privilege of the Writ of Habeas Corpus shall not be suspended, unless when in Cases of Rebellion or Invasion the public Safety may require it.

No Bill of Attainder or ex post facto Law shall be passed.

No Capitation, or other direct, Tax shall be laid, unless in Proportion to the Census or enumeration herein before directed to be taken.

No Tax or Duty shall be laid on Articles exported from any State.

No Preference shall be given by any Regulation of Commerce or Revenue to the Ports of one State over those of another: nor shall Vessels bound to, or from, one State, be obliged to enter, clear, or pay Duties in another.

No Money shall be drawn from the Treasury, but in Consequence of Appropriations made by Law; and a regular Statement and Account of the Receipts and Expenditures of all public Money shall be published from time to time.

No Title of Nobility shall be granted by the United States: And no Person holding any Office of Profit or Trust under them, shall, without the Consent of the Congress, accept of any present, Emolument, Office, or Title, of any kind whatever, from any King, Prince, or foreign State.

Section. 10.

No State shall enter into any Treaty, Alliance, or Confederation; grant Letters of Marque and Reprisal; coin Money; emit Bills of Credit; make any Thing but gold and silver Coin a Tender in Payment of Debts; pass any Bill of Attainder, ex post facto Law, or Law impairing the Obligation of Contracts, or grant any Title of Nobility.

No State shall, without the Consent of the Congress, lay any Imposts or Duties on Imports or Exports, except what may be absolutely necessary for executing it's inspection Laws: and the net Produce of all Duties and Imposts, laid by any State on Imports or Exports, shall be for the Use of the Treasury of the United States; and all such Laws shall be subject to the Revision and Controul of the Congress.

No State shall, without the Consent of Congress, lay any Duty of Tonnage, keep Troops, or Ships of War in time of Peace, enter into any Agreement or Compact with another State, or with a foreign Power, or engage in War, unless actually invaded, or in such imminent Danger as will not admit of delay.

Article. II.

Section. 1.

The executive Power shall be vested in a President of the United States of America. He shall hold his Office during the Term of four Years, and, together with the Vice President, chosen for the same Term, be elected, as follows:

Each State shall appoint, in such Manner as the Legislature thereof may direct, a Number of Electors, equal to the whole Number of Senators and Representatives to which the State may be entitled in the Congress: but no Senator or Representative, or Person holding an Office of Trust or Profit under the United States, shall be appointed an Elector.

The Electors shall meet in their respective States, and vote by Ballot for two Persons, of whom one at least shall not be an Inhabitant of the same State with themselves. And they shall make a List of all the Persons voted for, and of the Number of Votes for each; which List they shall sign and certify, and transmit sealed to the Seat of the Government of the United States, directed to the President of the Senate. The President of the Senate shall, in the Presence of the Senate and House of Representatives, open all the Certificates, and the Votes shall then be counted. The Person having the greatest Number of Votes shall be the President, if such Number be a Majority of the whole

Number of Electors appointed; and if there be more than one who have such Majority, and have an equal Number of Votes, then the House of Representatives shall immediately chuse by Ballot one of them for President; and if no Person have a Majority, then from the five highest on the List the said House shall in like Manner chuse the President. But in chusing the President, the Votes shall be taken by States, the Representation from each State having one Vote; A quorum for this Purpose shall consist of a Member or Members from two thirds of the States, and a Majority of all the States shall be necessary to a Choice. In every Case, after the Choice of the President, the Person having the greatest Number of Votes of the Electors shall be the Vice President. But if there should remain two or more who have equal Votes, the Senate shall chuse from them by Ballot the Vice President.

The Congress may determine the Time of chusing the Electors, and the Day on which they shall give their Votes; which Day shall be the same throughout the United States.

No Person except a natural born Citizen, or a Citizen of the United States, at the time of the Adoption of this Constitution, shall be eligible to the Office of President; neither shall any Person be eligible to that Office who shall not have attained to the Age of thirty five Years, and been fourteen Years a Resident within the United States.

In Case of the Removal of the President from Office, or of his Death, Resignation, or Inability to discharge the Powers and Duties of the said Office, the Same shall devolve on the Vice President, and the Congress may by Law provide for the Case of Removal, Death, Resignation or Inability, both of the President and Vice President, declaring what Officer shall then act as President, and such Officer shall act accordingly, until the Disability be removed, or a President shall be elected.

The President shall, at stated Times, receive for his Services, a Compensation, which shall neither be encreased nor diminished during the Period for which he shall have been elected, and he shall not receive within that Period any other Emolument from the United States, or any of them.

Before he enter on the Execution of his Office, he shall take the following Oath or Affirmation:—"I do solemnly swear (or affirm) that I will faithfully execute the Office of President of the United States, and will to the best of my Ability, preserve, protect and defend the Constitution of the United States."

Section. 2.

The President shall be Commander in Chief of the Army and Navy of the United States, and of the Militia of the several States, when called into the actual Service of the United States; he may require the Opinion, in writing, of the principal Officer in each of the executive Departments, upon any Subject relating to the Duties of their respective Offices, and he shall have Power to grant Reprieves and Pardons for Offences against the United States, except in Cases of Impeachment.

He shall have Power, by and with the Advice and Consent of the Senate, to make Treaties, provided two thirds of the Senators present concur; and he shall nominate, and by and with the Advice and Consent of the Senate, shall appoint Ambassadors, other public Ministers and Consuls, Judges of the supreme Court, and all other Officers of the United States, whose Appointments are not herein otherwise provided for, and which shall be established by Law: but the Congress may by Law vest the Appointment of such inferior Officers, as they think proper, in the President alone, in the Courts of Law, or in the Heads of Departments.

The President shall have Power to fill up all Vacancies that may happen during the Recess of the Senate, by granting Commissions which shall expire at the End of their next Session.

Section. 3.

He shall from time to time give to the Congress Information of the State of the Union, and recommend to their Consideration such Measures as he shall judge necessary and expedient; he may, on extraordinary Occasions, convene both Houses, or either of them, and in Case of Disagreement between them, with Respect to the Time of Adjournment, he may adjourn them to such Time as he shall think proper; he shall receive Ambassadors and other public Ministers; he shall take Care that the Laws be faithfully executed, and shall Commission all the Officers of the United States.

Section. 4.

The President, Vice President and all civil Officers of the United States, shall be removed from Office on Impeachment for, and Conviction of, Treason, Bribery, or other high Crimes and Misdemeanors.

Article III.

Section. 1.

The judicial Power of the United States, shall be vested in one supreme Court, and in such inferior Courts as the Congress may from time to time ordain and establish. The Judges, both of the supreme and inferior Courts, shall hold their Offices during good Behaviour, and shall, at stated Times, receive for their Services, a Compensation, which shall not be diminished during their Continuance in Office.

Section. 2.

The judicial Power shall extend to all Cases, in Law and Equity, arising under this Constitution, the Laws of the United States, and Treaties made, or which shall be made, under their Authority;—to all Cases affecting Ambassadors, other public Ministers and Consuls;—to all Cases of admiralty and maritime Jurisdiction;—to Controversies to which the United States shall be a Party;—to Controversies between two or more States;— between a State and Citizens of another State,—between Citizens of different States,— between Citizens of the same State claiming Lands under Grants of different States, and between a State, or the Citizens thereof, and foreign States, Citizens or Subjects.

In all Cases affecting Ambassadors, other public Ministers and Consuls, and those in which a State shall be Party, the supreme Court shall have original Jurisdiction. In all the other Cases before mentioned, the supreme Court shall have appellate Jurisdiction, both as to Law and Fact, with such Exceptions, and under such Regulations as the Congress shall make.

The Trial of all Crimes, except in Cases of Impeachment, shall be by Jury; and such Trial shall be held in the State where the said Crimes shall have been committed; but when not committed within any State, the Trial shall be at such Place or Places as the Congress may by Law have directed.

Section. 3.

Treason against the United States, shall consist only in levying War against them, or in adhering to their Enemies, giving them Aid and Comfort. No Person shall be convicted of Treason unless on the Testimony of two Witnesses to the same overt Act, or on Confession in open Court.

The Congress shall have Power to declare the Punishment of Treason, but no Attainder of Treason shall work Corruption of Blood, or Forfeiture except during the Life of the Person attainted.

Article. IV.

Section. 1.

Full Faith and Credit shall be given in each State to the public Acts, Records, and judicial Proceedings of every other State. And the Congress may by general Laws prescribe the Manner in which such Acts, Records and Proceedings shall be proved, and the Effect thereof.

Section. 2.

The Citizens of each State shall be entitled to all Privileges and Immunities of Citizens in the several States.

A Person charged in any State with Treason, Felony, or other Crime, who shall flee from Justice, and be found in another State, shall on Demand of the executive Authority of the State from which he fled, be delivered up, to be removed to the State having Jurisdiction of the Crime.

No Person held to Service or Labour in one State, under the Laws thereof, escaping into another, shall, in Consequence of any Law or Regulation therein, be discharged from such Service or Labour, but shall be delivered up on Claim of the Party to whom such Service or Labour may be due.

Section. 3.

New States may be admitted by the Congress into this Union; but no new State shall be formed or erected within the Jurisdiction of any other State; nor any State be formed by the Junction of two or more States, or Parts of States, without the Consent of the Legislatures of the States concerned as well as of the Congress.

The Congress shall have Power to dispose of and make all needful Rules and Regulations respecting the Territory or other Property belonging to the United States; and nothing in this Constitution shall be so construed as to Prejudice any Claims of the United States, or of any particular State.

Section. 4.

The United States shall guarantee to every State in this Union a Republican Form of Government, and shall protect each of them against Invasion; and on Application of the Legislature, or of the Executive (when the Legislature cannot be convened), against domestic Violence.

Article. V.

The Congress, whenever two thirds of both Houses shall deem it necessary, shall propose Amendments to this Constitution, or, on the Application of the Legislatures of two thirds of the several States, shall call a Convention for proposing Amendments, which, in either Case, shall be valid to all Intents and Purposes, as Part of this Constitution, when ratified by the Legislatures of three fourths of the several States, or by Conventions in three fourths thereof, as the one or the other Mode of Ratification may be proposed by the Congress; Provided that no Amendment which may be made prior to the Year One thousand eight hundred and eight shall in any Manner affect the first and fourth Clauses in the Ninth Section of the first Article; and that no State, without its Consent, shall be deprived of its equal Suffrage in the Senate.

Article. VI.

All Debts contracted and Engagements entered into, before the Adoption of this Constitution, shall be as valid against the United States under this Constitution, as under the Confederation.

This Constitution, and the Laws of the United States which shall be made in Pursuance thereof; and all Treaties made, or which shall be made, under the Authority of the United States, shall be the supreme Law of the Land; and the Judges in every State shall be bound thereby, any Thing in the Constitution or Laws of any State to the Contrary notwithstanding.

The Senators and Representatives before mentioned, and the Members of the several State Legislatures, and all executive and judicial Officers, both of the United States and of the several States, shall be bound by Oath or Affirmation, to support this Constitution; but no religious Test shall ever be required as a Qualification to any Office or public Trust under the United States.

Article. VII.

The Ratification of the Conventions of nine States, shall be sufficient for the Establishment of this Constitution between the States so ratifying the Same.

Done in Convention by the Unanimous Consent of the States present the Seventeenth Day of September in the Year of our Lord one thousand seven hundred and Eighty seven and of the Independance of the United States of America the Twelfth. In witness whereof We have hereunto subscribed our Names,

G°. Washington
Presidt and deputy from Virginia

Delaware
Geo: Read
Gunning Bedford jun
John Dickinson
Richard Bassett
Jaco: Broom

Maryland
James McHenry
Dan of St Thos. Jenifer
Danl. Carroll

Virginia
John Blair
James Madison Jr.

North Carolina
Wm. Blount
Richd. Dobbs Spaight
Hu Williamson

South Carolina
J. Rutledge
Charles Cotesworth

Pinckney
Charles Pinckney
Pierce Butler

Georgia
William Few
Abr Baldwin

New Hampshire
John Langdon
Nicholas Gilman

Massachusetts
Nathaniel Gorham
Rufus King

Connecticut
Wm. Saml. Johnson
Roger Sherman

New York
Alexander Hamilton

New Jersey
Wil: Livingston
David Brearley
Wm. Paterson
Jona: Dayton

Pennsylvania
B Franklin
Thomas Mifflin
Robt. Morris
Geo. Clymer
Thos. FitzSimons
Jared Ingersoll
James Wilson
Gouv Morris

In Convention Monday
September 17th 1787.

Present
The States of
New Hampshire, Massachusetts, Connecticut, Mr. Hamilton from New York, New Jersey, Pennsylvania, Delaware, Maryland, Virginia, North Carolina, South Carolina and Georgia.

Resolved,

That the preceeding Constitution be laid before the United States in Congress assembled, and that it is the Opinion of this Convention, that it should afterwards be submitted to a Convention of Delegates, chosen in each State by the People thereof, under the Recommendation of its Legislature, for their Assent and Ratification; and that each Convention assenting to, and ratifying the Same, should give Notice thereof to the United States in Congress assembled. Resolved, That it is the Opinion of this Convention, that as soon as the Conventions of nine States shall have ratified this Constitution, the United States in Congress assembled should fix a Day on which Electors should be appointed by the States which shall have ratified the same, and a Day on which the Electors should assemble to vote for the President, and the Time and Place for commencing Proceedings under this Constitution.

That after such Publication the Electors should be appointed, and the Senators and Representatives elected: That the Electors should meet on the Day fixed for the Election of the President, and should transmit their Votes certified, signed, sealed and directed, as the Constitution requires, to the Secretary of the United States in Congress assembled, that the Senators and Representatives should convene at the Time and Place assigned; that the Senators should appoint a President of the Senate, for the sole Purpose of receiving, opening and counting the Votes for President; and, that after he shall be chosen, the Congress, together with the President, should, without Delay, proceed to execute this Constitution.

By the unanimous Order of the Convention

G°. WASHINGTON—Presidt .
W. JACKSON Secretary.

The Bill of Rights & Amendments to the Constitution of the United States

Preamble to the Bill of Rights[1]

Congress Of The United States
begun and held at the City of New-York, on
Wednesday the fourth of March,
one thousand seven hundred and eighty nine

THE Conventions of a number of the States, having at the time of their adopting the Constitution, expressed a desire, in order to prevent misconstruction or abuse of its powers, that further declaratory and restrictive clauses should be added: And as extending the ground of public confidence in the Government, will best ensure the beneficent ends of its institution:

RESOLVED by the Senate and House of Representatives of the United States of America, in Congress assembled, two thirds of both Houses concurring, that the following

---

[1] On September 25, 1789, Congress transmitted to the state legislatures twelve proposed amendments, two of which, having to do with Congressional representation and Congressional pay, were not adopted. The remaining ten amendments were ratified effective December 1 5, 1791 and became the Bill of Rights. The amendment concerning Congressional pay was ratified on May 7, 1992, becoming the Twenty-Seventh Amendment to the Constitution

Articles be proposed to the Legislatures of the several States, as Amendments to the Constitution of the United States, all or any of which Articles, when ratified by three fourths of the said Legislatures, to be valid to all intents and purposes, as part of the said Constitution; viz.t .

ARTICLES in addition to, and Amendment of the Constitution of the United States of America, proposed by Congress, and ratified by the Legislatures of the several States, pursuant to the fifth Article of the original Constitution.

FREDERICK AUGUSTUS MUHLENBERG
Speaker of the House of Representatives.
JOHN ADAMS, Vice-President of the United States, and President of the Senate.

ATTEST,

JOHN BECKLEY, Clerk of the House of Representatives. SAM. A. OTIS, Secretary of the Senate.

Amendments to the Constitution of the United States of America

Amendment I.

Congress shall make no law respecting an establishment of religion, or prohibiting the free exercise thereof; or abridging the freedom of speech, or of the press; or the right of the people peaceably to assemble, and to petition the Government for a redress of grievances.

Amendment II.

A well regulated Militia, being necessary to the security of a free State, the right of the people to keep and bear Arms, shall not be infringed.

Amendment III.

No Soldier shall, in time of peace be quartered in any house, without the consent of the Owner, nor in time of war, but in a manner to be prescribed by law.

Amendment IV.

The right of the people to be secure in their persons, houses, papers, and effects, against unreasonable searches and seizures, shall not be violated, and no Warrants shall issue, but upon probable cause, supported by Oath or affirmation, and particularly describing the place to be searched, and the persons or things to be seized.

Amendment V.

No person shall be held to answer for a capital, or otherwise infamous crime, unless on a presentment or indictment of a Grand Jury, except in cases arising in the land or naval forces, or in the Militia, when in actual service in time of War or public danger; nor shall any person be subject for the same offence to be twice put in jeopardy of life or limb; nor shall be compelled in any criminal case to be a witness against himself, nor be deprived of life, liberty, or property, without due process of law; nor shall private property be taken for public use, without just compensation.

Amendment VI.

In all criminal prosecutions, the accused shall enjoy the right to a speedy and public trial, by an impartial jury of the State and district wherein the crime shall have been committed; which district shall have been previously ascertained by law, and to be informed of the nature and cause of the accusation; to be confronted with the witnesses against him;

to have compulsory process for obtaining witnesses in his favor, and to have the assistance of counsel for his defence.

Amendment VII.

In Suits at common law, where the value in controversy shall exceed twenty dollars, the right of trial by jury shall be preserved, and no fact tried by a jury, shall be otherwise re-examined in any Court of the United States, than according to the rules of the common law.

Amendment VIII.

Excessive bail shall not be required, nor excessive fines imposed, nor cruel and unusual punishments inflicted.

Amendment IX.

The enumeration in the Constitution of certain rights shall not be construed to deny or disparage others retained by the people.

Amendment X.

The powers not delegated to the United States by the Constitution, nor prohibited by it to the States, are reserved to the States respectively, or to the people.

Amendment XI.[2]

The Judicial power of the United States shall not be construed to extend to any suit in law or equity, commenced or prosecuted against one of the United States by Citizens of another State, or by Citizens or Subjects of any Foreign State.

Amendment XII.[3]

The Electors shall meet in their respective states, and vote by ballot for President and VicePresident, one of whom, at least, shall not be an inhabitant of the same state with themselves; they shall name in their ballots the person voted for as President, and in distinct ballots the person voted for as Vice-President, and they shall make distinct lists of all persons voted for as President, and of all persons voted for as Vice-President, and of the number of votes for each, which lists they shall sign and certify, and transmit sealed to the seat of the government of the United States, directed to the President of the Senate;—The President of the Senate shall, in the presence of the Senate and House of Representatives, open all the certificates and the votes shall then be counted;—The person having the greatest number

---

[2] The Eleventh Amendment was ratified February 7, 1795.

[3] The Twelfth Amendment was ratified June 15, 1804.

of votes for President, shall be the President, if such number be a majority of the whole number of Electors appointed; and if no person have such majority, then from the persons having the highest numbers not exceeding three on the list of those voted for as President, the House of Representatives shall choose immediately, by ballot, the President. But in choosing the President, the votes shall be taken by states, the representation from each state having one vote; a quorum for this purpose shall consist of a member or members from two-thirds of the states, and a majority of all the states shall be necessary to a choice. [And if the House of Representatives shall not choose a President whenever the right of choice shall devolve upon them, before the fourth day of March next following, then the Vice-President shall act as President, as in the case of the death or other constitutional disability of the President —][4] The person having the greatest number of votes as Vice-President, shall be the Vice-President, if such number be a majority of the whole number of Electors appointed, and if no person have a majority, then from the two highest numbers on the list, the Senate shall choose the Vice-President; a quorum for the purpose shall consist of two-thirds of the whole number of Senators, and a majority of the whole number shall be necessary to a choice. But no person constitutionally ineligible to the office of President

---

[4] Superseded by Section 3 of the Twentieth Amendment

shall be eligible to that of Vice-President of the United States.

Amendment XIII.[5]

Section 1.

Neither slavery nor involuntary servitude, except as a punishment for crime whereof the party shall have been duly convicted, shall exist within the United States, or any place subject to their jurisdiction.

Section 2.

Congress shall have power to enforce this article by appropriate legislation.

Amendment XIV.[6]

Section 1.

All persons born or naturalized in the United States and subject to the jurisdiction thereof, are citizens of the United States and of the State wherein they reside. No State shall make or enforce any law which shall abridge the privileges or immunities of citizens of the United States; nor shall any State deprive any person of life, liberty, or property, without

---

[5] The Thirteenth Amendment was ratified December 6, 1865

[6] The Fourteenth Amendment was ratified July 9, 1868.

due process of law; nor deny to any person within its jurisdiction the equal protection of the laws.

Section 2.

Representatives shall be apportioned among the several States according to their respective numbers, counting the whole number of persons in each State, excluding Indians not taxed. But when the right to vote at any election for the choice of electors for President and Vice President of the United States, Representatives in Congress, the Executive and Judicial officers of a State, or the members of the Legislature thereof, is denied to any of the male inhabitants of such State, being twenty-one years of age, and citizens of the United States, or in any way abridged, except for participation in rebellion, or other crime, the basis of representation therein shall be reduced in the proportion which the number of such male citizens shall bear to the whole number of male citizens twenty-one years of age in such State.

Section 3.

No person shall be a Senator or Representative in Congress, or elector of President and Vice President, or hold any office, civil or military, under the United States, or under any State, who, having previously taken an oath, as a member of Congress, or as an officer of the United States, or as a member of any State legislature, or as an executive or judicial officer of any State, to support the Constitution of the United States, shall have engaged in insurrection or rebellion against the same, or given aid or comfort to the enemies thereof. But Congress may by a vote of two-thirds of each House, remove such disability.

Section 4.

The validity of the public debt of the United States, authorized by law, including debts incurred for payment of pensions and bounties for services in suppressing insurrection or rebellion, shall not be questioned. But neither the United States nor any State shall assume or pay any debt or obligation incurred in aid of insurrection or rebellion against the United States, or any claim for the loss or emancipation of any slave; but all such debts, obligations and claims shall be held illegal and void.

Section 5.

The Congress shall have power to enforce, by appropriate legislation, the provisions of this article.

Amendment XV.[7]

Section 1.

The right of citizens of the United States to vote shall not be denied or abridged by the United States or by any State

---

[7] The Fifteenth Amendment was ratified February 3, 1870.

on account of race, color, or previous condition of servitude.

Section 2.
The Congress shall have power to enforce this article by appropriate legislation.

Amendment XVI.[8]

The Congress shall have power to lay and collect taxes on incomes, from whatever source derived, without apportionment among the several States, and without regard to any census or enumeration.

Amendment XVII.[9]

The Senate of the United States shall be composed of two Senators from each State, elected by the people thereof, for six years; and each Senator shall have one vote. The electors in each State shall have the qualifications requisite for electors of the most numerous branch of the State legislatures.

When vacancies happen in the representation of any State in the Senate, the executive authority of such State shall

[8] The Sixteenth Amendment was ratified February 3, 1913.

[9] The Seventeenth Amendment was ratified April 8, 1913.

issue writs of election to fill such vacancies: Provided, That the legislature of any State may empower the executive thereof to make temporary appointments until the people fill the vacancies by election as the legislature may direct.

This amendment shall not be so construed as to affect the election or term of any Senator chosen before it becomes valid as part of the Constitution.

Amendment XVIII.[10]

[Section 1.

After one year from the ratification of this article the manufacture, sale, or transportation of intoxicating liquors within, the importation thereof into, or the exportation thereof from the United States and all territory subject to the jurisdiction thereof for beverage purposes is hereby prohibited.

Section 2.

The Congress and the several States shall have concurrent power to enforce this article by appropriate legislation.

---

[10] The Eighteenth Amendment was ratified January 16, 1919. It was repealed by the Twenty-First Amendment, December 5, 1933.

Section 3.

This article shall be inoperative unless it shall have been ratified as an amendment to the Constitution by the legislatures of the several States, as provided in the Constitution, within seven years from the date of the submission hereof to the States by the Congress.]

Amendment XIX.[11]

The right of citizens of the United States to vote shall not be denied or abridged by the United States or by any State on account of sex. Congress shall have power to enforce this article by appropriate legislation.

Amendment XX.[12]

Section 1.

The terms of the President and the Vice President shall end at noon on the 20th day of January, and the terms of Senators and Representatives at noon on the 3d day of January, of the years in which such terms would have ended if this article had not been ratified; and the terms of their successors shall then begin.

---

[11] The Nineteenth Amendment was ratified August 18, 1920.

[12] The Twentieth Amendment was ratified January 23, 1933.

Section 2.

The Congress shall assemble at least once in every year, and such meeting shall begin at noon on the 3d day of January, unless they shall by law appoint a different day.

Section 3.

If, at the time fixed for the beginning of the term of the President, the President elect shall have died, the Vice President elect shall become President. If a President shall not have been chosen before the time fixed for the beginning of his term, or if the President elect shall have failed to qualify, then the Vice President elect shall act as President until a President shall have qualified; and the Congress may by law provide for the case wherein neither a President elect nor a Vice President elect shall have qualified, declaring who shall then act as President, or the manner in which one who is to act shall be selected, and such person shall act accordingly until a President or Vice President shall have qualified.

Section 4.

The Congress may by law provide for the case of the death of any of the persons from whom the House of Representatives may choose a President whenever the right of choice shall have devolved upon them, and for the case of the death of any of the persons from whom the Senate may choose a Vice President whenever the right of choice shall have devolved upon them.

Section 5.

Sections 1 and 2 shall take effect on the 15th day of October following the ratification of this article.

Section 6.

This article shall be inoperative unless it shall have been ratified as an amendment to the Constitution by the legislatures of threefourths of the several States within seven years from the date of its submission.

Amendment XXI.[13]

Section 1.

The eighteenth article of amendment to the Constitution of the United States is hereby repealed.

Section 2.

The transportation or importation into any State, Territory, or Possession of the United States for delivery or use therein of intoxicating liquors, in violation of the laws thereof, is hereby prohibited.

---

[13] The Twenty-First Amendment was ratified December 5, 1933

Section 3.

This article shall be inoperative unless it shall have been ratified as an amendment to the Constitution by conventions in the several States, as provided in the Constitution, within seven years from the date of the submission hereof to the States by the Congress

Amendment XXII.[14]

Section 1.

No person shall be elected to the office of the President more than twice, and no person who has held the office of President, or acted as President, for more than two years of a term to which some other person was elected President shall be elected to the office of President more than once. But this Article shall not apply to any person holding the office of President when this Article was proposed by the Congress, and shall not prevent any person who may be holding the office of President, or acting as President, during the term within which this Article becomes operative from holding the office of President or acting as President during the remainder of such term.

Section 2.

This article shall be inoperative unless it shall have been ratified as an amendment to the Constitution by the

---

[14] The Twenty-Second Amendment was ratified February 27, 1951.

legislatures of threefourths of the several States within seven years from the date of its submission to the States by the Congress.

Amendment XXIII.[15]

Section 1.
The District constituting the seat of Government of the United States shall appoint in such manner as Congress may direct:

A number of electors of President and Vice President equal to the whole number of Senators and Representatives in Congress to which the District would be entitled if it were a State, but in no event more than the least populous State; they shall be in addition to those appointed by the States, but they shall be considered, for the purposes of the election of President and Vice President, to be electors appointed by a State; and they shall meet in the District and perform such duties as provided by the twelfth article of amendment.

Section 2.
The Congress shall have power to enforce this article by appropriate legislation.

---

[15] The Twenty-Third Amendment was ratified March 29, 1961.

Amendment XXIV.[16]

Section 1.

The right of citizens of the United States to vote in any primary or other election for President or Vice President, for electors for President or Vice President, or for Senator or Representative in Congress, shall not be denied or abridged by the United States or any State by reason of failure to pay any poll tax or other tax.

Section 2.

The Congress shall have power to enforce this article by appropriate legislation.

Amendment XXV.[17]

Section 1.

In case of the removal of the President from office or of his death or resignation, the Vice President shall become President.

Section 2.

Whenever there is a vacancy in the office of the Vice President, the President shall nominate a Vice President

---

[16] The Twenty-Fourth Amendment was ratified January 23, 1964.

[17] The Twenty-Fifth Amendment was ratified February 10, 1967.

who shall take office upon confirmation by a majority vote of both Houses of Congress.

Section 3.

Whenever the President transmits to the President pro tempore of the Senate and the Speaker of the House of Representatives his written declaration that he is unable to discharge the powers and duties of his office, and until he transmits to them a written declaration to the contrary, such powers and duties shall be discharged by the Vice President as Acting President.

Section 4.

Whenever the Vice President and a majority of either the principal officers of the executive departments or of such other body as Congress may by law provide, transmit to the President pro tempore of the Senate and the Speaker of the House of Representatives their written declaration that the President is unable to discharge the powers and duties of his office, the Vice President shall immediately assume the powers and duties of the office as Acting President.

Thereafter, when the President transmits to the President pro tempore of the Senate and the Speaker of the House of Representatives his written declaration that no inability exists, he shall resume the powers and duties of his office unless the Vice President and a majority of either the principal officers of the executive department or of such other body as Congress may by law provide, transmit within four days to the President pro tempore of the Senate and the Speaker of the House of Representatives their written declaration that the President is unable to discharge the powers and duties of his office. Thereupon Congress shall decide the issue, assembling within forty-eight hours for that purpose if not in session. If the Congress, within twenty-one days after receipt of the latter written declaration, or, if Congress is not in session, within twenty-one days after Congress is required to assemble, determines by two-thirds vote of both Houses that the President is unable to discharge the powers and duties of his office, the Vice President shall continue to discharge the same as Acting President; otherwise, the President shall resume the powers and duties of his office.

Amendment XXVI.[18]

Section 1.
The right of citizens of the United States, who are eighteen years of age or older, to vote shall not be denied or abridged by the United States or by any State on account of age.

---

[18] The Twenty-Sixth Amendment was ratified July 1, 1971.

Section 2.

The Congress shall have power to enforce this article by appropriate legislation.

Amendment XXVII.[19]

No law, varying the compensation for the services of the Senators and Representatives, shall take effect, until an election of Representatives shall have intervened.

---

[19] Congress submitted the text of the Twenty-Seventh Amendment to the States as part of the proposed Bill of Rights on September 25, 1789. The Amendment was not ratified together with the first ten Amendments, which became effective on December 15, 1791. The TwentySeventh Amendment was ratified on May 7, 1992, by vote of Michigan.